Our God Reigns

The Praise and Worship Collection

Contents

A *J. Aaron Brown & Associates* Publication
in association with

HAL LEONARD PUBLISHING CORPORATION

Home Office:
960 East Mark Street
Winona MN 55987

National Sales Office:
8112 West Bluemound Road
Milwaukee WI 53213

ISBN 0-88188-618-1

Writer Index

BROWN BANNISTER
160 Praise

DAVID BARONI
78 Keep The Flame Burning

BOBBY BINION, JR.
94 We Shall Behold The King

DAVID BINION
295 O For A Thousand Tongues
94 We Shall Behold The King

NILES BOROP
236 His Word Will Stand
328 It Is Good
247 Proclaim The Glory Of The Lord
168 Rejoice In The Lord
192 Sing With Joy
315 Via Dolorosa
347 Wherever You Are Is Holy Ground

LARRY BRYANT
23 Desires Of My Heart, The
271 In Your Hands
172 It Was Enough
334 Nothin' Improves My Day

PATTI BURTON
285 Greatly Rejoice

WENDELL BURTON
285 Greatly Rejoice
305 Who He Is

CINDY CARLSON
36 Dreamer's Dream
320 Thanksong

PETE CARLSON
36 Dreamer's Dream
320 Thanksong

GARY CHAPMAN
70 Arms Of Love

MORRIS CHAPMAN
100 Bethlehem Morning
164 Come And Sing Praises
65 Worthy Is The Lamb

CHRIS CHRISTIAN
148 No Other Name But Jesus

CLAIRE CLONINGER
252 Even The Mountains Praise You
50 Part-Time Servant
83 Simple Song For A Mighty God
226 Spirit Wings
55 Surrender

JOHN RANDOLPH COX
138 Above It All

BILLY CROCKETT
222 Lord Is Lifted Up, The

ANDREW CULVERWELL
232 Cover Me

BEVERLY DARNALL
176 Bless You Lord

JOHN DARNALL
176 Bless You Lord

GERON DAVIS
133 Holy Ground

MICHAEL FOSTER
226 Spirit Wings

JOHN FOWLER
331 Let Us Draw Near

WILLIAM GAITHER
196 We Are So Blessed

GLORIA GAITHER
196 We Are So Blessed

AMY GRANT
70 Arms Of Love
60 Thy Word

PAM MARK HALL
290 Blessing
88 Now And The Not Yet, The
160 Praise

WALT HARRAH
206 No More Night

DOROTHY HAUSCH
152 Peace

REID HAUSCH
152 Peace

JAMES HOLLIHAN
240 We Will Stand

MIKE HUDSON
339 Our God Reigns

JOE HUFFMAN
152 Peace

NEAL JOSEPH
252 Even The Mountains Praise You

GREG LAUGHERY
290 Blessing

DWIGHT LILES
236 His Word Will Stand
247 Proclaim The Glory Of The Lord
192 Sing With Joy

GREG MASSANARI
164 Come And Sing Praises

PHILL McHUGH
142 He Will Meet My Needs
180 Love Found A Way
108 Power In Jesus Name

GARY McSPADDEN
200 Jesus Lord To Me
148 No Other Name But Jesus

RICHARD MULLINS
276 O Come All Ye Faithful
4 Sing Your Praise To The Lord

CONNIE NELSON
78 Keep The Flame Burning

Sing Your Praise to the Lord

Words and Music by
RICHARD MULLINS

Adapted from J.S.Bach's Fugue No.2 in C minor, WTC Vol.I

In a steady four, with excitement ♩=88

life to you, the life goes on ___ and so must the song. You got-ta

mad - d'ning crowd, as you once were ___ be-fore you heard ___ the song. You got-ta

sing a -gain the song born _ in your soul when you _ first gave your

let them know the truth is a - live _____ to shine up-on the way so may-be

heart to Him, sing His prais - es. Once more sing your

they can go,

sing your prais-es. Once more sing your just how much good that it's gon-na do _ ya. Just to

sing, sing, __ sing, let me hear ya now, sing, sing, __ sing. __

O Magnify the Lord

Words and Music by MELODIE TUNNEY
and DICK TUNNEY

mag - ni - fy, __ O mag - ni - fy __ the Lord __ with me, __ and
(2) wor - ship Him, __ O wor - ship Christ, __ the Lord __ with me, __ and

14

El-Shaddai

MICHAEL CARD

JOHN THOMPSON

18

CODA

Through the years — you made — it clear — that the time —

— of Christ — was near, _____ though the peo - ple could - n't see —

22

The Desires of My Heart

Words and Music by
LARRY BRYANT

26

The de-sires___ of my___ heart._____

Let Me Give

Words and Music by
LESLIE PHILLIPS

down___ to the ver - y small.___

1.

2. Nev - er ___

rit.

How Majestic Is Your Name

Words and Music by
MICHAEL W. SMITH

O Lord,__ our Lord,__ how ma-

Dreamer's Dream

Words and Music by
PETE and CINDY CARLSON

With sensitivity

Verse 1 What start - ed as a dream - er's dream,

Verse (2) an - swers I've been told be - fore, don't ap -

38

joy?_____ Well I

Coda

that You are mak - ing me,_____

that You are mak - ing me._____

Cornerstone

Words and Music by
LEON PATILLO

In four, with a 'Hebrew' feel

Hosanna

Words and Music by DEBORAH D. SMITH and
MICHAEL W. SMITH

48

Part - Time Servant

CLAIRE CLONINGER

KEITH THOMAS

With purpose $\quad$ = 66

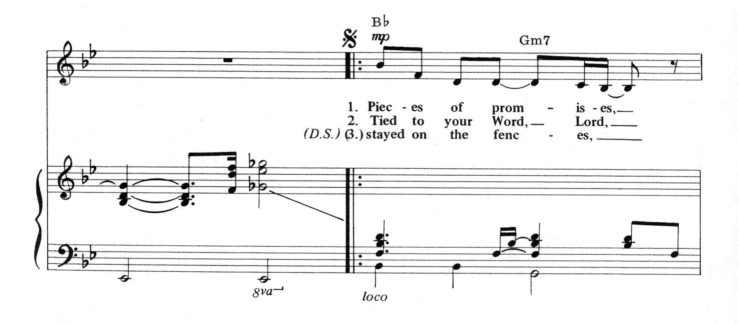

1. Piec - es of prom - is - es, ___
2. Tied to your Word, ___ Lord, ___
(D.S.) (3.) stayed on the fenc - es, ___

parts of a prayer, ___ no real ___ com-mit - ment ___ to
just by a thread, ___ the need in ___ my heart, and ___ the
Lord, lin - g'ring still, ___ just on ___ the edge of ___ my

3.I've

Coda

Oh.

From this day__ on my__ life's an__ o - pen door,__ I won't be your

54

part - time   ser - vant _____   an - y - more.

Surrender

CLAIRE CLONINGER

BILL PURSE

Thy Word

AMY GRANT

MICHAEL W. SMITH

Based on Psalm 119:105

With meaning ♩ = 80

*Guitar chords
are up a half step*

Thy Word is a lamp un-to my feet and a light un-to my path.

cued note 4th time

(Now)

1. When I feel a - fraid, think I've lost my way,
2. I will not for - get your love for me and yet my

still you're there right be - side me. And
heart for - ev - er is wan - der - ing.

noth - ing will I fear as long as you are near.
Je - sus be my guide, and hold me to your side, and

D.S. al Coda
2nd time to

Please be near me to the end.
I will love you to the end.

Noth- ing will __ I __ fear as __ long as you __ are __ near.

Please be near me to the end. _____

Thy Word is a lamp __ un - to __ my __ feet __ and a __

light _____ un - to ____ my path.

Worthy Is the Lamb

Words and Music
MORRIS CHAPMAN

Arms of Love

Words and Music by
**GARY CHAPMAN,
MICHAEL W. SMITH
and AMY GRANT**

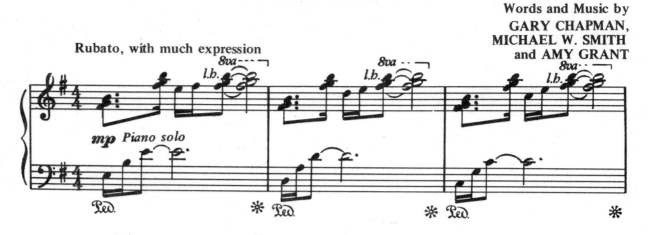

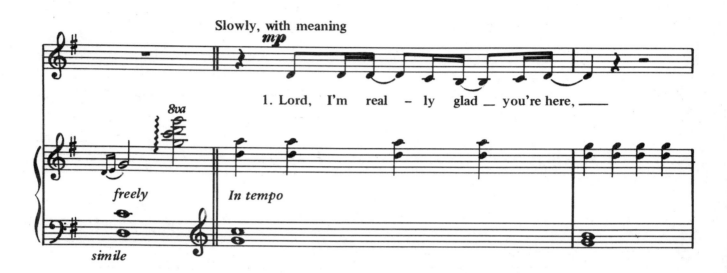

1. Lord, I'm real - ly glad __ you're here, __

I hope you feel __ the same __ when you __ see all __ my fear, and how I've

72

I Dedicate All My Love to You

Words and Music by TERI DESARIO PURSE
and BILL PURSE

With much expression ♩=116

1. Just when the dark - ness a - round___ me seemed black - est, You
2. Just when my dreams___ turned to night - mares,___ You woke me

called, but I was so blind ___ to You; So
up, ___ born to a new ___ day; Then

Chorus:

76

Keep the Flame Burning

Words and Music by
DAVID BARONI and
CONNIE NELSON

With conviction ♩ = 84

1. Lord I find __ my-self need-ing you like I
2. Chil-dren He knows __ what you're go-ing through He suf-fered

nev - er have _____ be - fore. _____ In
more than you'll _____ ev - er know. _____ Well He's

Simple Song for a Mighty God

CLAIRE CLONINGER   KEITH THOMAS

Moderately slow ballad ♩ = 62

with pedal

1. He spread the stars a-cross the night, and built His pal-ace in the heav-ens.
2. Wrapped in robes of light, He brought cre-a-tion in-to be-ing,

The Now and the Not Yet

Words and Music by
PAM MARK HALL

With hope ♩ = 120

(D.S.) 1. No long - er
la.) 2. No long - er

89

glo - ry,— wrapped up— in— His glo -

3rd time to 🔂 **1.**

- ry. We— will be like— Him— for

we shall see— Him as— He is.—

2.

(La la la la la la la But I'm caught in be - tween— the

now and the not__ yet. Some-times it seems__ like for-

ev - er and ev - er that I've been reach - ing__ to be

all that I am, __ but I'm on - ly a few__ steps

near - er,__ yet I'm near -

92

We Shall Behold the King

Words and Music by
DAVID BINION and
BOBBY BINION, JR.

hold _____ the King!

2. He gave His
3. Soon time shall

life,   leav - ing   a   prom - ise _____   of
cease,   end - ing   all   sor - row, _____   bro - ken

hope _____ for all who be - lieve. _____
hearts _____ will no long - er bleed. _____

Bethlehem Morning

Words and Music by
MORRIS CHAPMAN

106

Power in Jesus Name

Words and Music by GREG NELSON
and PHILL McHUGH

110

1. On the cross He died, shamed and cru-ci-fied — was hope gone for the blind and the lame? No, the Christ did rise, came and dwelt in-side, fill-ing dis-ci-ples with power in His name. We have

2. We, the Bride of Christ, must be armed to fight, Sa-tan's ar-my as-sails us each day. In the bat-tle hour we must know our power, all that we have in His glo-ri-ous name. We have

2nd time D.S. al Coda

⊕ Coda

power, power, pow - er in Je - sus'

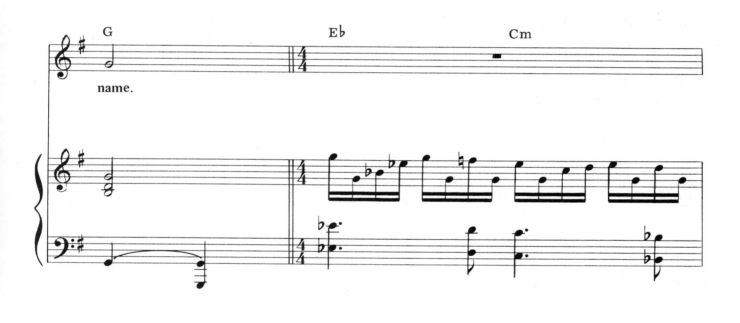

name.

rit.

Jehovah

Words and Music by
GEOFFREY P. THURMAN

Flowing, with purpose ♩ = 138

*(C♯in bass)

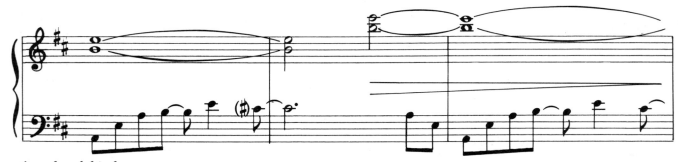

✳ end pedal in bass

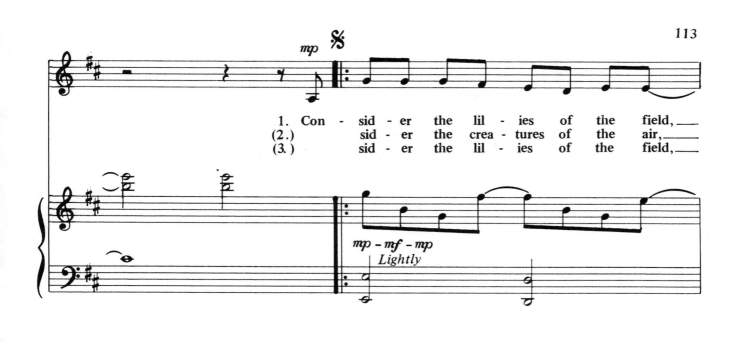

1. Con - sid - er the lil - ies of the field, ___
(2.) sid - er the crea - tures of the air, ___
(3.) sid - er the lil - ies of the field, ___

cued notes: 2nd time

for Sol - o - mon dressed in roy - al robe ___
for all of the dia - monds in all ___
for how much more does He love His own, ___

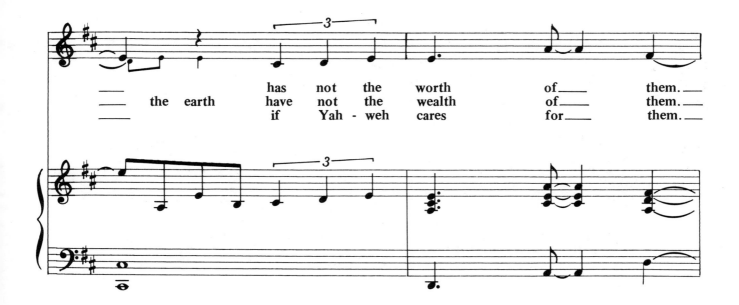

the earth has not the worth of ___ them. ___
the earth have not the wealth of ___ them. ___
if Yah - weh cares for ___ them. ___

Con - sid - er the lil - ies of the field,___
Con - sid - er the crea - tures of the air,___
Con - sid - er the crea - tures of the air,___

He takes af - ter each and ev - 'ry need.___
Je - ho - vah loves them with ten - der hands.
He takes af - ter each and ev - 'ry need.___

Leave all your cares be - hind;
He knows your ev - 'ry care;
If we ask Him for bread,

vah I love you so, and Je-sus I want you to know

Ah

all you've done for me to set me free, I'll

1,3.

nev - er let you go. And Je - ho -

2.

D.S.

nev - er let you go.

3. Con -

nev - er let_ you_ go._____ And

Je - ho - vah, I love_ you so,___

loco

(C♯ *in bass*)

and_ Je - sus_ I ___ want

(C♯ in bass)

you to know_____ all_ you've done_

118

*(C# in bass)

Repeat and fade | Optional ending

Nev - er let you

(C♮ in bass)

(B in bass)

tenuto

L.H.

ritard

Hosanna!

Words and Music by
TRICIA WALKER

1. Je - sus of__ Na - za - reth, son of a__
2. Teach - er of__ par - a - bles, work - er of__

car - pen-ter, born in a sta - ble, yet born to be__
mir - a - cles, Sav - ior of sin - ners, have mer - cy on__

124

So Praise Him

Words and Music by JIM WEBER and
MICHAEL W. SMITH

Repeat 1st time only

1. When tri - als come and life is out of hand, and sad con -
2. The bat - tle is - n't eas - y now my friend, and all your

fu - sion and pain are all you know;
sor - row has backed you to the wall;

128

Great Is the Lord

Words and Music by
MICHAEL W. SMITH and DEBORAH D. SMITH

132

Holy Ground

Worshipful ♩=69

Words and Music by
GERON DAVIS

1. As I walked through the door
(2) pres - ence there is joy

I sensed His
be - yond

pres - ence,_____
meas - ure,_____

and I knew this was a
and at His feet peace of

pres - ence, on ho - ly ground.

2. In His__ ground.

Let__ us__

praise_____

Je - sus now,_____

Above It All

Words and Music by
JOHN RANDOLPH COX and
CHRIS WATERS

1. He hum-bled him-self____ as a man,____ mocked, re-jec-ted, des-pised;____
2. He walked__ down the al-leys and streets,____ served the poor and the lost;____

He Will Meet My Needs

Words and Music by GREG NELSON and
PHILL McHUGH

No Other Name But Jesus

Words and Music by GARY
McSPADDEN, CHRIS CHRISTIAN
and BILLY SMILEY

The First and Last, Be - gin-ning and the End,___ He was the
The One who said, "I am the great I Am,"___ ___ then

King who made the com-mon man His friend,___ there is no oth - er name;___
gave Him - self, the sac - ri - fice for man,___ there is no oth - er name;___

Let ev - 'ry tongue pro- claim___ and sing the name of
Let ev - 'ry tongue pro -claim___ and sing the name of

Je - sus, mag-ni - fy___ and praise the name___ of Je - sus;___ No

Peace

Words and Music by DOROTHY HAUSCH, REID HAUSCH
and JOE HUFFMAN

Let's Lift Him High

Words and Music by GREG NELSON and
JUSTIN PETERS

1. Je - sus is the Son of God,— He's all the hope— in me; Cre - a - tor and— Re - deem - er of my—
2. Born a babe in Beth - le - hem,— He came to set— men free; With faith in God,— He died— on Cal - va -

Praise

With excitement ♩=120

Words and Music by PAM MARK HALL and
BROWN BANNISTER

Praise to the Fa - ther, Praise to the Son, _____ Praise to the Spir - it, the Three in One; Praise to the

162

Come and Sing Praises

Based on Psalm: 29:1-2

Words and Music by
MORRIS CHAPMAN and GREG MASSANARI

166

Rejoice in the Lord

Words and Music by
NILES BOROP and
JIM WEBER

With conviction ♩.=56 (Steady two)

1. Hon - or the Lord, with all your heart, let your words glo - ri -
(2) hon - or You, Lord, with all our hearts, let our words glo - ri -

right - eous, re - joice in the Lord and

sing! Lift up your voice in an

of - f'ring of praise and re - joice,_____ re -

1. joice in our King!_____

It Was Enough

Words and Music by
LARRY BRYANT

174

that You died for me.

2. He said,

that I died for you."

Bless You Lord

Words and Music by JOHN DARNALL
and BEVERLY DARNALL

Love Found a Way

With meaning

Words and Music by
PHILL McHUGH
and GREG NELSON

182

Great is Your Faithfulness

Words and Music by
DAWN RODGERS and
TRICIA WALKER

Lord I Need You Now

Words and Music by BILLY SPRAGUE
and JIM WEBER

Sing With Joy

Words and Music by NILES BOROP
and DWIGHT LILES

Like the an - gel hosts _ a - bove,_ re - joice a - round _ His throne._ Ev - 'ry

3rd time to

liv - ing thing,_ lift up your voice and sing with

joy be - fore_ the Lord!

We Are So Blessed

WILLIAM and GLORIA GAITHER

GREG NELSON

Jesus Lord to Me

Words and Music by
GREG NELSON and GARY McSPADDEN

No More Night

Based on Hebrew 11:13-16 and Revelation 21

Words and Music by
WALT HARRAH

1. The time-less

The Heavens are Telling

Words and Music by
TRICIA WALKER

213

Sing for Joy

Rhythmically, with excitement!

♩ = 92

Words and Music by PAUL SMITH, DENISE SMITH
and KEITH THOMAS

1. Hearts   that were fro - zen once__ in si -
2. So   let there be__ no hes - i - ta-

The Lord Is Lifted Up

KENNY WOOD

BILLY CROCKETT

Spirit Wings

Words and Music by
CLAIRE CLONINGER and MICHAEL FOSTER
INSPIRED BY A POEM BY GUYON

maj - es - ty, you lift me up, (lift me up) you

car - ry me on your Spir - it wings.

You car - ry me_ up - on_your Spir - it wings._

Vocal ad lib

Repeat and fade

232

Cover Me

Words and Music by
ANDREW CULVERWELL

His Word Will Stand

Moderato ♩=69

Words and Music by NILES BOROP
and DWIGHT LILES

1. Some say it's myth and leg - end, one more
(2) lis - ten to the voic - es of a

book up - on the shelf, but the mes - sage it___ con - tains___ can-not be
world caught___ up in fear, for the Word of God___ pro - claims___ the vic - to -

Though no man be - lieves— Him, still

God will— be true. His prom-ise is sure, His love will en - dure, and for -

ev - er— His Word will— stand.

2. Don't stand. His Word will

We Will Stand

(You're My Brother, You're My Sister)

RUSS and TORI TAFF

JAMES HOLLIHAN

Proclaim the Glory of the Lord

Words and Music by NILES BOROP and
DWIGHT LILES

Even the Mountains Praise You

CLAIRE CLONINGER

NEAL JOSEPH

Relaxed half-time feel ♩ = 60

1. As I lift my voice— to You,
2. ___ The ear - ly morn - ing rain,___

You, and I must be part of the song. So

come let us bring ev-'ry praise— to the King,— pro-claim-ing that Je-sus is

Lord.

D.S. al Coda

Coda

And as the earth— spins on,— more and more

I must be part of the song. So come let us bring ev'ry praise

to the King, pro - claim - ing that Je - sus is

Lord.

I Need to Feel Your Touch Again

Words and Music by
TRICIA WALKER

Moderately in four ♩ =116

When I — woke this morn - ing — to start an - oth - er day
— My days have been so bu - sy,— too ma - ny things to do,

260

Lord, I need_ to feel ___ your touch_ a - gain, I need to be_ as- sured___ you're still my friend. I need to know_ the pow - er ___ in your blood that clean - ses

Be Still My Soul

Words and Music by
RUSS and TORI TAFF

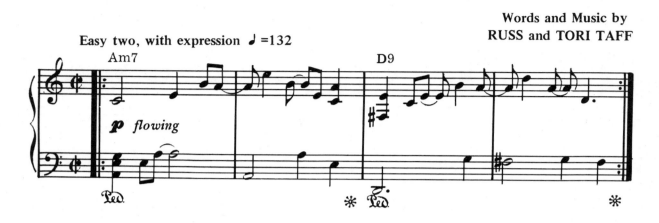

In Your Hands

Words and Music by BILLY SIMON
and LARRY BRYANT

O Come All Ye Faithful

Words and Music by
RICHARD MULLINS

With excitement ♩. = 63

1. O

Greatly Rejoice

Moderately ♩=126

Words and Music by PATTI BURTON and
WENDELL BURTON

287

Blessing

Words and Music by
PAM MARK HALL and
GREG LAUGHERY

trou - bles He_ will take_ you._ On His Word you can_ de - pend,_ that He

nev - er will for - sake_ you._ He'll stick clos - er than_ a friend._

May His mer - cy_ al - ways keep_ you_ from the

wick- ed and_ the vain - heart- ed peo - ple who de - ceive_ you,_ and

May His Spir-it al-ways keep— you,— from the
crook-ed deeds of night,— as He strength-ens you with pow-er,— and
leads you to the light.————————— May God—

Repeat and fade

O For a Thousand Tongues

Words and Music by
DAVID BINION

298

Sing the Glory of His Name

Excited! ♩=80

Words and Music by
TRICIA WALKER

1. Come and see___ the works___ of God,___ awe-some to___ the
2. Come and hear___ what God___ has done:___ heal-ing bod - y,

Sing _____ the glo - ry of

His   name!

Who He Is

Words and Music by
WENDELL BURTON

To the Praise of His Glorious Grace

Words and Music by MICHAEL W. SMITH
and DEBORAH D. SMITH

1 Let us praise the One who chose us,

Let us thank the One who knows us;

Via Dolorosa

Words and Music by BILLY SPRAGUE
and NILES BOROP

the nar - row street;
up - on__ His head;
But the crowd__
And He bore__

pressed in to see,__
with ev - 'ry step __
a man con - demned to die__
the scorn of those who cried__

on Cal - va - ry.__
out for His death.__

1.

2.

2. He was __ Down the

318

Thanksong

Words and Music by PETE CARLSON and
CINDY CARLSON

When I Hear Your Name

Words and Music by
DAWN RODGERS

With a feeling of awe ♩ = 84

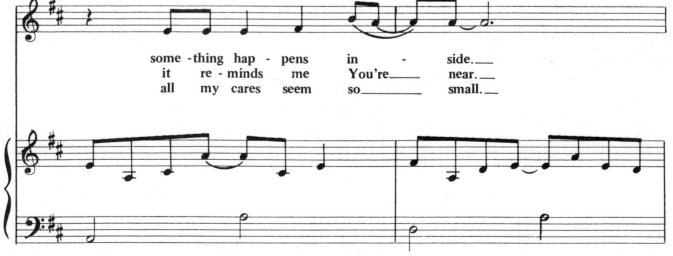

1. When - ev - er I hear Your___ name,
(2.) hear Your___ name,
D.S. (3.) hear Your___ name,

some - thing hap - pens in - side.___
it re - minds me You're___ near.___
all my cares seem so_____ small.___

I know that my heart can____ change,
I know that Your love re - mains,
I know that You're Lord of____ me,

so there's no need to _____ hide. _____
when there's no one else_____ _____ here. _____
____ since You're Lord of _____ _____ all. _____

____ And I ____ know you____
____ All the____ know things I ____
____ And my____ heart will____

It is Good

Words and Music by JIM WEBER and
NILES BOROP

330

Let Us Draw Near

JOHN FOWLER

TRICIA WALKER and JOHN FOWLER

name,   All   power   and   glo - ry   to   Your

name.

Nothin' Improves My Day

(Better than Praisin' Him)

Words and Music by LARRY BRYANT

1. I can get so both - ered by things that mat - ter least,
2. Have you ev - er no - ticed the days that seem the worst,

Our God Reigns

Words and Music by MICHAEL W. SMITH
and MIKE HUDSON

1. Lie down and sleep___ to - night,
2. Go out in faith___ to - day,

let your soul find___
bring praise to His___

there is light in our dark - ness,

2nd time to

our God___ reigns!

Baruch Hashem Adonai

Words and Music by
DAWN ROGERS and
TRICIA WALKER

1. Who am___ I to be part of Your peo-ple, the ones that are called by Your
2. How can a stran - ger, a rem - nant of na-tions, be - long to this roy - al___
3. How could You show me such boun - ti - ful mer-cy by tak - ing the life of the
4. Praise to You, Je - sus, the veil has been part-ed, and what once was se - cret is

Wherever You Are Is Holy Ground

Words and Music by
JIM WEBER and NILES BOROP

We Will Glorify

With dignity ♩ =69

Words and Music by TWILA PARIS

1. We will glo - ri - fy the
(2) ho - vah reigns in